*Likely*

Wick Poetry First Book Series
Maggie Anderson, Editor

*Already the World*
Victoria Redel

GERALD STERN, JUDGE

*Likely*
Lisa Coffman

ALICIA SUSKIN OSTRIKER, JUDGE

)

# Likely

*Poems by*
Lisa Coffman

The Kent State
University Press
*Kent, Ohio, &*
*London, England*

Library of Congress Catalog Card Number 96-11211
ISBN 0-87338-554-3 (cloth)
ISBN 0-87338-555-1 (pbk.)
Manufactured in the United States of America


04  03  02  01  00  99  98  97  96      5 4 3 2 1


The Wick First Book Series is sponsored by the Stan and Tom Wick Poetry Program and the Department of English at Kent State University.

Composed in Adobe Minion
by Diana Gordy at The Kent State University Press.
Text designed by Will Underwood.
Cover and binding designed by Diana Gordy.
Printed and bound by Thomson-Shore, Inc.

*Library of Congress Cataloging-in-Publication Data*

Coffman, Lisa, 1963–
        Likely : poems / by Lisa Coffman.
            p.      cm.—(Wick poetry first book series)
        ISBN 0-87338-554-3 (cloth : alk. paper). —ISBN 0-87338-555-1 (pbk. : alk. paper)
        I. Title.    II. Series.
    PS3553.O412L55    1996                                              96-11211
    811'.54—dc20                                                        CIP


British Library Cataloging-in-Publication data are available.

for the five Wright sisters
  Lois, Missy, Lorellen, Una, Sherry

# CONTENTS

Part IV

# ACKNOWLEDGMENTS

I thank the editors of the following magazines in which these poems, or versions of these poems, first appeared: "Romeo Collision," *The Beloit Poetry Journal;* "In Fraser's Mills," *The Cincinnati Review;* "Cold Sunday," "About the Pelvis," "The Road to Canso," *The Drunken Boat;* "Rogue Gene," "Rapture," "In Envy of Migration," "Walking Under a Straw Hat in Tuscon," *Kestrel;* "Learning the Butterfly," "February Landscape with Moons and Hearts," "For Sheila's Julia," "Girl/Spit," *New Millennium Writings;* "Maps," "Pulled Down," *Now and Then;* "For Najeema, 6, Who Admitted to Hitting Renee," *Painted Bride Quarterly;* "The Products of Hog," "The Simple Day," *River City;* "Likely," "Beaded Tongue and Groove," *The Southern Review;* "The Small Town," "Brother Ass," *West Branch.*

"The Cicadas," "The Boy with the Bluberries," and "Courage, or One of Gene Horner's Fiddles" first appeared in the anthology *All Around Us: Poems from the Valley* (1996).

I thank the following people, who provided encouragement and support at various times during the writing of this book: Una Coffman, Karin Cornils, Chris Kaufman, Richard Kenney, Donna Mote, Karl Patten, and Bob Taylor. And most of all I thank Gus Hedberg.

Many thanks to Maggie Anderson and Alicia Ostriker for their close readings and wise suggestions on the text.

I am very grateful to Bo Bartlett, who made the beautiful painting for *Likely*'s cover.

Fellowships from The Pew Charitable Trusts, the Pennsylvania Council on the Arts, and the Stadler Center for Poetry at Bucknell University supported me while I wrote many of these poems.

I

# LIKELY

Magnolia bloom can sex the air
until one thinks for long blanknesses
only *magnolia, magnolia.*
The tree shakes with the climbing of two girls.
The taller, stretched among four branches
looks up, carrying a knife.
The other settles at a lesser place
and thinks of falling. Magnolia
withers if touched. The petals
spot where the fingers were, then darken,
spoiling the smell. A girl raised
to be her daddy's boy knows to reach,
slowing and slowing the hand until
it wavers with the flower.
She cuts the slight wood at the stem,
tips to her a color of things hidden—
skin at the lifted clothes, or the shining
averted face of a woman undressing.
The younger girl will run alongside with the news.
The flower floats all night in a glass,
the kitchen lit in other places by the moon.

## GIRL / SPIT

She presses her dark lips
in a pleased way, as if she has said
the word *whiskey* again, or tucked
into a corner of her mouth a grass blade
which she briefly squatted and chose
before standing, and with a slap
to her back pockets, slouched
into the length of herself.

It's the hook-thinness of her smile
that draws something like the beaded
metallic chain of a lamp
down my spine and stomach, toward the pucker
her smile has pushed to its corner—
the flutter of that cheek
working down on itself, working spit,
and finding its own taste sweet.

# MEMLING'S VIRGIN

For love of her, he exaggerated.
And for love of her, forgot that he did.

And for love, permitted himself to attend her,
to smooth her brow and fan the hair spilling on the rich pale robe
toward her long hands that always lay restfully.

And for her pleasure selected
the headband beaded with five-pearl flowers,
brocading across the chest shallow as a girl's,
a gold trinket box, the Holy Book, an apple small as a plum.
And for love of her had her look at none of it.

And put no one near her but the child
who would say, as she knew, *Woman what have I to do with thee?*

Working before her daily
he shaped the eyes that were turned down, the narrow upper lip
she sealed in her composure on the lower full one,

and when he could do no more—
as the executioner lifted the elegant jointed spear—

he turned her away
and drew the shawl over her head.
And, perhaps against his own desire, disclosed
the profile hardened in the constriction of grief—
then gave the tears a milky light, like pearls.

# CHEERLEADERS

Out of the American provinces
regarded by many as exile
one is born into—
evolves the oddity of a girl
to whom her own opinions pose a danger
yet able to shout, pinioned
in the execution of a complex-figured leap
before any number of audience, local, or from nearby towns.

Admitting "their attitude is like that of strippers,"
admit a scrubbed citric innocence to the sex.
No Venus grins here from the foam, curl ends tweaked water-dark:
the hair fanned across the inwardly groaning boy's fourth-period desk
has been ironed flat or flipped up,
the hairless lotioned calves end in sock folds,
the chest is topped demurely with a carpet letter.

As for the bruited away-bus escapades of sex:
these are more often exaggerations
in the nature of all town troubadours.
The intent is, rather, "to be kissproof:
put on lipstick, then have someone
powder your lips through a piece of tissue. Do
not inhale." Not admired by majestic-thighed women
passing in and out of steamroom steam
are the somnolent voices roused to staccato, single drawn word starting
low ending loud, childish bell still to *go OH go OH*
as the lead girl takes her hands from her hips
among all eight waiting in identical postures
and puts the bunny-ear shape of her sneaker to an in-place prancing
or strikes the wooden court boards hard
until the stands start ringing back.

Even admitting the ingenuity of their pleats
that allow the skirt to extend straight from the waist,
and the athletic rigor required for certain jumps,
no one accuses cheerleaders of usefulness:
they are discarded at the end of high schools
excluded from cabinet meetings and businesses,

yet, while it is known
"there are no women like that, anywhere!"
as the young photographer cried, home
from retouching hair and blemishes
on women already exemplary for beauty,

his girlfriend and sisters in the magazine-
littered living room
merely looked at him, then went on with their reading.

## WEATHER

When I sit teaching among my red-lipped girls sugaring to ripeness
among the flushed necks prideful as mine has been
and feel in myself only the new wish
to lie down in the earliest dark and turn my face

or when I go among pleasured women filling with first child, oh
when I want to go over what is gone and done
then I come to my high room that faces the river
and the wide light the river moves ceaselessly under.

# THE SMALL TOWN

*Are not two sparrows sold for a farthing? And one of them shall*
*not fall on the ground without your Father.*
*But the very hairs on your head are all numbered.*

—*Matthew 10:29, 30*

Its summer is a boy in red swim trunks
head shaved like his Daddy's lawn
and who has never wept at a whipping.
And who kicks in the walls of his sand tunnel
and must be unburied and whacked
out of that still sleep by a hysterical mother.
Its summer is the crotch-shaped joining
of Emory into Clinch into one brown river
laced with child pee, cut by boat propellers
and upstream chemical dumpings. And it is the fish
the river receded from and the fish flesh rotted
to the spine that gleams like a knife.
And the sex-stricken Baptist Youth Choir
singing of God's Grace. And the car that tips
past ruined rail on the bridge and the grinning
mask of the drunk's face beginning to scream.
And the dinner potatoes whipped in the pot,
the forked roast, and steam off the plates.
And the hidden cove's rope knotted for swinging,
boys on the sloped bank, and the curled-up toes
and *iiiieeee* of the fall. And it is the languorous
black snake, having survived the garden hoe.
And the man who sees God and is told
to dig at a fence post. He finds a tiny stone cross
for his dead son and holds this up in church.
And the girl who bends to her first cock,
sword curve unzipped from the boy's rented tuxedo pants
while her lavender wrist corsage sweetens the dark car.
And the boy who sighs as one going to sleep.
And the softball field lights coming on
over government houses at Flourmill Flats.
And the lights of houses on the mountains.

And a woman hoeing the tangled bean rows near sunset
when the river has lost all color and is only shine.
And she grumbles at a husband who plants but won't weed.
And the river drags a fermented smell with it.
And the powerful flanks of the mountains darken first.

# RAPTURE

What is the gear that turns this world?
Bright now, the wall of the east sky like honey
    church chimes off red tenement bricks
    off humped roads where the vans slam down their loading ramps
    subway clap in the beams and the window frames shaking.

What's left of the night's in the shadows of things
precise and solid: the cornice tops
    the shadow of that branch so hard I could lift it.

The white-smocked fish-market man bends from the waist
    receiving and flinging boxes from the truck ramp
butt above his head, weight swung
    from bent leg to straight leg now bent
head down, grunting and hugging the boxes—
    the silver, hacked bodies of fish in the window.

Another man sits on an upturned box outside the grocer's
    legs planted on each side of his box like a storyteller.
The motion of his hands breaks and strips beans
    never seeming to put a bean down and reach for the next one:
    always the green scrap of bean in his hand.
And the rhythm of stripping is the rhythm of mending
                   or weaving a cane-bottom seat.

If the mountains will let me back,
if they will let me back and give me a small house:
    yellow light in winter when the mountains are gray
    the brittle spiked pine scent splayed over me in winter.

Now the red-headed boy on our street comes out of his house.
    He has grown up:
I first saw him going to Catholic school with his small head of hair
 slicked back
Once he pushed two boys on our stoop and said *I can kill both you guys.*
Yesterday he tucked his shirt in and crossed the street
              where the girls idle in the blue evening.
He looked worried:
           wet dreams and erections have humbled him.

I have thought I might be a hater of Jews
    and I have never met a black man without being afraid.
    I have never met a woman without being afraid.

My brother squealed in the yard. I made up games.
We pulled the dog by a stick; if we fell, he pulled us.
When my brother went in his pants, our mother
      took the shit and smeared it on each of his cheeks.
    I remember the pitch his cry went into.
The dog is old now and staggers and has cataracts like white stars.

Whatever it is, it must be very basic,
we must turn of a piece, or the turning is no good.
We must turn of a piece
                 but there is nothing so good
as the row of furrows cut in the earth,
as the gold block of cheese on the dark shelf.

# LEARNING THE BUTTERFLY

I like that it is violent.
I like its indiscretion
of noise in the low, tiled room.
I like being a new animal,
shoulders first breaking the water,
jaws closing as I go down.
It is a metaphor for my life
since there is never any balance:
either my bones are pulling me under
or my body, at the last, like a wing beat
is throwing me free of the water.
The instructor says, *go slowly,*
but my double dolphin kicks are my trumpets
I'm the gold car in the parade of triumph,
I'm the train and its oncoming scream—

I like the other side
and being reduced
to the husking noises of breathing,
then to lift out and pad away, light,
elaborate as an open cage.

# BEADED TONGUE AND GROOVE

Homage to a kind of loving, its best pleasure
hidden, over and over on the walls, the ceiling,
around the porch, where three cane rockers wave
in the longer breeze or storm's approach.
The surface boards, narrow like all thoroughbreds,
would be severe, but for the bead
welling at each fit, a suggestion of things that change
in the lightest touch, very small pearl buttons
or the rounded outer corners of the mouth.
Here, pattern holds up a wall of pieces
within pattern: heat in bent wires off the roads,
lit edges of dark blind slats, and the over-and-under
sprawl of the lovers, resting, almost breathless.
Now their eyes begin to focus and turn in the dark room.
Now he is saying *beaded tongue and groove*
as he has run a hand across it sometime or driven nails in evenly.
Now she answers the name refers to sex, as speech likes to.
They lie in the last heaviness before moving,
like water massed fullest before it rocks or breaks into waves.
Now memory begins its ordering, in one or the other, *once
I was.* They lie a bit longer, then rise.

II

# THE BOY WITH THE BLUEBERRIES

Conceding the city hurt his simple head,
he goes home, into the blue mountains
that secure the horizon, and roll on,
side to side, touching, like a herd.

And he becomes cheap labor timbering
where woods lock darker onto what was town.
"that over there was the big garden" and so forth,
foundation showing like some lunar rim.

Beach slipped from the knife still smells like fish;
the mottled trail betrays the limping stag.
Houses close on the road in apparent watchfulness:
the clever ones plead to leave, then leave,

sometimes come back. Approaching them, he says,
failing to despise what will not have him,
"If you are here tomorrow I can bring berries.
I can find you all the berries you'd want."

"Thank you—we go today." As though they'd turned
after—what? some whistle, snatch of color,
and stared and could not find it,
he leaves them wanting where they were not wanting.

# PULLED DOWN

We came from Pickett—land down under the mountain.
We left our houses empty and shuttered with light.
For three days to the brick yards at Robbins,
another to the new shaft above Glenmary,
our wagons swung like the windy fields we left.
The wages we came for we called *public works.*
And some men were lucky, worked near the entrance, the good air,
some in the mill that razed unblemished timber,
but others each day in the shaft rooms
broke and sent out the coal that sealed them in.
A man who brought bad news came home, bathed twice,
saying *I can't go as I am.* Women
bent among their staked vines in gardens;
our Mason's emblem praised the strong right arm.
And we had peacocks in our yards for something pretty
and the foreman's daughter in her pretty fat.
When our companies left, we pulled down company houses
and built other houses from them, which have fallen,
and The Hundreds, and the tipple, and coke ovens,
so many names to tell you for gone things.
The Hiwassi Land Company has planted it all in pine
and sprayed the oaks so they died standing
and stand, a peeled, monumental white
unlike our land: green stroke that hooks, pulls down.

No one of us can ever be alone—
the Cincinnati line stopped here
some fifty years, then left for good—
there's a trailer hooked into grandmother's yard,
the great house itself sits in weeds
and hay baled for the horse tied to the porch:
the once-town's shrunk to Route 27.

Glenmary's on one side of the road.
Take the twine from the door and let us see her,
the couch where she lay, arm to her head.
Summer: one child's in the cellar for lying,
four shout with the high voices of running
where the yard grows dark. Out back
the garden raises itself, inch and bust.

Her twentieth year. Sick near to death
she grows big in her coats, as the iron pot
boiling hard when black Sukie comes
through the smoke and cold of November
with a long razor. One of the children
runs when the pigs scream, ducks her head
as though her father held her, runs harder.

The room where all but the last child were born
has fallen through to the floor below:
the ivy has tiny hooks, but they work.
*We'd stand on the tracks and dare each other*
*to jump last when the trains got close.*
Their grandmother's hotel has eighteen rooms
eighteen salesmen, wash basins and stands,

all of it lost. The railroad named Glenmary.
Girls lined up for the evening train:
a platform of the prettiest daughters,
the velvet cheeks and coat collars
of Glenmary, unincorporated, now home
to the most pitiful dog, most prosperous ticks:
green, fat as class rings.

Who lives by the garden? An old cousin, crazy,
won't let visitors through. Who's in the trailer?
Renters, they're letting the old house fall. Who's
in the woods? Two men, cutting trees for tax money.
And the hotel? There are only foundations,
things that cry the same thing all day:
fly and cricket, the thirsty snake.

# M A P S

*for Curtis O. Roberson (1906–1994)*

*In 1960, my grandmother's cousin Curtis Roberson was one
of two men assigned by the Appalachian Power Company to find
and move all graves in a four-county area near Roanoke,
Virginia, that would subsequently be flooded by the Smith
Mountain Dam Project. Over the next two-and-a-half years,
Curtis and his partner Herbert Taylor, both APCo employees
since the 1930s, supervised the relocation of 1,361
graves.*

1.

Rely on old maps: they hold a place
just as our faces retain who we have been
and will shine with us now in who we will be,
so dearly does the flesh love us—

its palm lines are said to be a map
of our wanderings under the stars,
then into the root-starred earth.

2.

*Ah, lo—*
What was the little song you would sing at evening
free from the burden of work
when all paths led endlessly into the green ease of the world?

*lo lo Lord—*
Did you sing of the good Christians going to heaven?
Of the sweet one leaned forward on the porch
until all but your white shirt was gone in the dark?

*Lord, Lord, Lord—*
Or did you sing of the forgotten dead
pocketed in the green hills of Bedford County
of Franklin and Roanoke Counties?

Some later resting above the flexing rim of Smith Mountain Lake
some dissolving with the soft lake bed
most the Company moved—

some having left as witness loose buttons,
teacups alongside a thigh, wedding bands,
some unmarked, attended by periwinkle

said to grow of its own accord over the dead.
But by then you were getting on,
a good Company man, instructed to watch

each moved to a two-by-two-by-one-foot box.

3.

My father is photographed above lit-up Roanoke Valley,
age fourteen. This face shows up later in my brother.
Curtis is photographed with his prize roses.
Smith Mountain Dam floods more light into Roanoke.
Maps are changed. And so on.
Proof of the grave is a stain left in the earth
*from the corpse, the clothes it wore. Sure, girl*
*all the grave holds is a little colored soil*
he says, peace of old men on him,
straightens his prize roses. Old maps, inaccurate,
still tell the sites of graves. But flesh maps
what we lose, and all traces of a body's music.

# ROGUE GENE

Rogue gene bides its time in me,
carrier, perhaps an heir. I don't mean
mama's fanny on papa's skinny body—
that's genetic mix. Nor the temper
that threw great-grandmother down the stairs—
we all got that. Rogue gene shows up
once a thousand years, maybe used once,
maybe Asiatic: the hobbled concubine
or he the knuckle scraper who bowed and straightened
in the shadows of stones, while the saber-toothed
roared like a big rock hitting bottom.
Rogue gene may have been raped into our line:
a pirate who pissed over his ship's side on a fine day.
I like to think it apocalyptic: a warlord gene,
but it could be facial tic, or a six-fingered hand.

We branched and branched like hands.
Some of us ended up in alleys, threatening to tear the lips off
     someone else.
Some of us ended up prayer-doubled, moaning over sinful birth.
Some plodded in underground prisons, half forgetful of family
     voices.
And I, quilt of thousands,

remember the tiger
that almost ate us
remember the stranger
faced us so long back of the house before vanishing
remember the snake bite and the drunken dreams it brought
remember the water on the dress before the baby
remember the fever that took us that summer
nothing but the wall, at last, to look at

There's no way of knowing my family:
height, gait, speech—or presence of the rogue gene.

# THE PRODUCTS OF HOG

*(Cincinnati, 1849)*

Hog loosed in a cornfield is the happiest creature
eating his last five days. That's the part
they don't know. Only nearing the city—
ten slaughterhouses it's grown to—
does the front of the drove try to turn off
however you shout or apply the sticks.
We pack them so they stand after they're hit:
a hammer with a pick breaks the skull.
I swing it two-handed—it takes my breath—
and the stronger my arms the better it is
for the hog. We try not to lose blood
by the pens: there's money in that.
And fat, hooves, the scraped bristles
find a market so good the firm pays
hog owners for slaughter rights.
Five hundred thousand head processed
in Cincinnati this year. I don't count
what I've hit, but by how long
my arms hurt, by the liniments, doses of whiskey.

# ON A MILL WORKER IN ROCKWOOD

*for Thomas Hayes*

He'd come home and put his face in his hands,
whiskey and chair by the kitchen door,
while your Mamaw fixed supper he never ate
and small at the table, you watched his bent back.

Whiskey and chair by the kitchen door,
he'd lurch to the stove and pile in more wood
and small at the table, you watched his bent back,
heat bright in the room like hell preached in church.

He'd lurch to the stove and pile in more wood,
face closed as the fist he hit you with,
heat bright in the room like hell preached in church
while your Mamaw whispered you were excused.

Face closed as the fist he hit you with,
"Damn HEAT" he'd cry and kick open the door
while your Mamaw whispered you were excused,
the night shiny black when his shift was up.

"Damn HEAT" he'd cry and kick open the door,
sit coughing and swearing as you went to bed,
the night shiny black when his shift was up:
he'd come home and put his face in his hands.

# THE ROAD TO CANSO

From Canso came the rumor: mackerel were running,
the net pattern of green-black mackerel
that would jump in a boat—
water thick with mackerel (or the absence of mackerel).

Three took a truck to Canso. The driver spoke:
"This road is some curvy." Left it at that
till lunch. Denied that his dog bites: "There! There!
Put your hand out to her!" Black flies bite the dog
and bloody the sides of the trembling cow.
The three dawdled on their way to Canso
and ate cod and chips in a Canso trailer.

There is a tradition of marriage in Scots houses:
the daughters stay married but the sons come home.
In every neighborhood one or two make it:
he not a bad drinker, falling and sleeping
in the grass by his house,
she with the eye of a running hen,
and bachelor uncles all brought in to dinner.

Out of the other marriages a great party is made
along the logging road, where logging trucks
stop for nothing but a truck
but cars pull in at houses and the lights come on.
"Son of a whore! show us those mackerel!"

Canso land accommodates the fog,
and trees are black, like a widow's skirt
in Canceau, capital for a New World.
A great ship stopped in a Canso inlet
let down nets and swallowed all the mackerel:
so went the story up and down the logging road.

The town's most famous bachelor
slips from a party on the second or third day,
sleeps it off, wears Chinese silk patterned slippers,
does dishes, calls his brother's widow,
then finds the party. In this way
he has lived to be quite old.

# IN FRASER'S MILLS

A red-haired man lives at home with his mother
in Fraser's Mills. Their roof slopes like the hill side
where the trees gap. From the road at the hill's foot
someone would have to direct your eyes ("the fir
that leans on another? now over: spruce shaped
on top like a big hat? now up: there's the house")
if you're new to those woods. The bulky eagle,
who falls first when he flies, is hard to make out
in his perch: dark and white in the darker trees.

The red-haired man would like to jump from a tree.
Spruce shapes work into a head in those winters.
He hitches a ride to town for beer. Can't read.
Can't drive, then. Except tractors at haying time.
And one leg, to spite him, stopped growing. The state
sends a monthly check and paid for the dentist
who ordered all his teeth pulled. His old mother
crosses herself when they're driven past graveyards.
He hides his beer in an abandoned cabin.

If you are new to those woods, the red-haired man
will turn his face from you, questions in his eyes
bright as tears. If he's drunk, he'll try to offend:
"*you* are the strangest stranger ever came here"
and he lights up a smoke in your living room.
If you are the friend of a friend, he will talk.
If you are brooding, he waits out on your steps.
Calls, "WE ALL GET THAT WAY." Summer's haying left
a roar in his ears, an itch. Hearing's going.

III

# THE QUALITY OF SWEETNESS IN MEN

Like the enforced size of the bonsai,
although not so cultivated; commonly
confused with what is called womanly;
      this show of desire
shows itself shyly, or if the man as man has been
      discarded—as with the four

      waiting since dawn by the oversized
double glass doors for the warm library
to let them in—he may give freely
      of what is left him:
in a voice so sorrowing it sings "you drink you drug
      you feeling this" one of them

      mourns for all four. In old men, as
the soul moves nearer death, there emerges
the childish wish to share what amazes,
      pain also. One calls
"since the stroke I cannot wave this arm to you!" takes up
      the withered arm, holds it close.

      And of the young men marched to the front
that winter, light spooling off their faces'
down, very few returned. His face is
      almost disfigured
with pleasure: the children playing move like little birds!
      He stops, tranced, the ex-soldier.

      Otherwise permitted when fetching,
rescuing, in the respite of strangers,
or in love before enduring love enters,
      this seducing pace
of the heart's is guarded against as if a thief, this
      open hand intending peace.

# FEVER

White curtain, bedpost, crossed wrists
in the silt color of evening, the traffic far off,
burned dry, licking my lips over and over
as the room is turned to the slow machinery of fever.
In the next room he reads. The lit doorway
makes the quilt on my knees a ridge:
I'm a kingdom, a patient field of stitches
behind a mountain, safe—
the quilt my mother gave me. Pink crosspieces
the color for a girl. State flowers chain-stitched
to each square, the embroidery knots
denoting seed: warm dense-packed
center of the sunflower, the sour life-smell
of my father's garden, how far I'm gone—
another hand on my forehead in the shrinking dark
meaning *home*  this pain   hot river   forgetful

# COLD SUNDAY

*(Fort Augusta Museum, Pennsylvania)*

1.

Thief and father of us, why did you steal
the milk glass beads from the Indian's grave?
All your thieving came to is a museum case
and what will he wear in the heaven the beads were meant for?

Winter early and the furnace broken.
We drove to be driving. Crows laughed hard
at a scarecrow and settled near corn.
We came home in the bruise-colored light and lay down.

*Who owned the fort owned the river—*
thus the curator. But every thirty
years the Susquehanna floods
past dikes, past sandbagged walls above the sunken towns.

2.

Love, your hands are fine nets that close and open about me.
Lay your glasses with their false light on the bedside table.
Open the shirt's button row downwards and quickly
then the dark-colored pants with the *shhh* of being shucked off.
Lie here, and we will be warm. We are winter's harvest.

# IN ENVY OF MIGRATION

1.

The new American Fabricare laundromat
built from an out-of-business ribs place
keeps its lights on until late
and fans flicking underneath the lights
and women outside leaned against the thick storefront glass
and children orbiting those women's laps.

2.

I was home when the starlings crossed over.
The flock settled and lifted off the yard as it passed.
Always they were calling ahead, behind.
They seemed to have great news.
I think it is pride iridescing their black wings,
pride of the Many-in-One,
like the stand of oaks when the wind starts
or the many impeccable bones of the foot.

3.

The femur prepares for journey
for years: long mineral additions in secret.
Then it can slacken over the shapes of car seats
or chairs in offices
or porch stairs during a joblessness,
or I have seen it part the china color of streetlight
under one left walking when the night is on us.

## WALKING UNDER A STRAW HAT IN TUSCON

I believed in the horizontal lightning.
I believed it ran over the earth like a jackal
aimed at my knees, or chest
turned hurtable forever when I turned twelve.
I believed I would die far from my mother.
I saw the saguaro split on the mountain:
black glazed its wound. On the ground
the skin still tried to crawl off
in the skyline churned red after sundown.
Then I saw the sky strike itself. Only itself.
Strike sideways, like a human spite
or the grieving body of a tall woman,
this lightning that never touches down.

But the fear hasn't left me.
Even when I walk. Even when I sing and walk.

# FIVE SAPPHICS TO A FRIEND
## ON RETURNING FROM A TRIP

Friend, I'm home. It's already autumn here, seems
odd. The trip?—I hate that I cry in airports.
When I saw him waiting, I started. He, un-
able to cry, smoked.

\*\*\*

Hear a secret: while he was planting trees he
found the bird the cat had just killed. He laid it
under loosened roots of an oak to bury.
Only I saw him.

\*\*\*

Grown, you'll start your childhood. Or try to. No more
turning music up when he hit her, beating
doors to stop them. Quiet and play: you'll try, now
their house has fallen.

\*\*\*

*No,* the knife word, bolted me fast, legs kicking.
*No:* I gave it fat off my face to eat. I'm
*no,* the word, I'm both in one body: sighing
victim, knife thrower.

\*\*\*

Blame ambition, upbringing. Here I walk the
dike bank when I'm bad off. And you? A ruined
tower bears the name of our town. Guards watch the
footbridge from Trenton.

## FEBRUARY LANDSCAPE WITH MOONS AND HEARTS

The mind comes to the morning glittering like snow
and the mind thinking of death is like snow in blue shadows

but when the body thinks of death, it leans nearer
to the tune of the dark earth coursing with sleepers.

Who loves me releases imprints
of tiny hearts into the air from his hands.
For his valentine I made a funeral handbill
of the great fighter *gallo del cielo*
who the songs all agree rose up time after time
moonlight threading the first crack through the beak.

I dreamed my love passed by bowed like a sickle,
heel showing through his torn shoe like a sickle moon.

# ROMEO COLLISION

### 1.

Say there are two emotions, love or fear,
one casting out the other like the winner
in rock-paper-scissors. Some mornings (this one)
fear takes up the bed and windows, takes up
my human shape and walks it room to room—
when I'm alone, so later can't be proved.
Related subject: X let her husband's girlfriend,
who boasted to beforehand, begin
to make love with her. Some party guests looked on.
Of the two asleep, feet touching, their pattern—
hips cupped, or opening opposite, sweat
strong on the sheets by morning—we have let
their habits shelter us, shoulder or bureau
in outline, nights. X knows. I know.

### 2.

*See where the weeds are pink,* I show the child,
her chin dug in the seat back. Outside Newark
the Meadowlands swung, heavy-tipped, between track
sections, car glass, canisters. Your good eye

assembled what I love: a pelt-
colored land cut by bridges, cracking tower's
fire. Or found one afternoon, in a bar,
a child's shoes thrown among petals

of a torn-up rose. The fish, huge,
*with two great dead rotten eyes*
you came running to report, stride
mismatched, a tall man's, two kinds of music.

Unlike you, I can sit and stare,
for hours, see nothing, like a passenger.

3.

Take the char taste of fight to bed,
or better, defer till morning with beer, rum,
then throw it up. Not that I slept.
(Recall the acres near my parents' home

ruined in fire, dead trees like knives
upright for years.) One night while I burned,
wanting the house still, the last lights
in the kitchen out, I heard father and son

go over lessons, the deep voice first with *walk*
or *blue*, the other, soft, as in question,
answering *azul . . . jugar . . .* they seemed to talk
like two long familiar, who didn't listen,

spoke when the other stopped, but at a peace,
one asking *will you*, the other *yes*

4.

"Better dead than in some basement." The locksmith
shows how the bolt will fit. To sleep, I use
left-over medicine, locks that take keys
both sides of the door. The alleged stayed with

his mother, not two months out of prison
when he *raped a city* (read: *black*) *woman, beat
her with a pipe* The next woman, white,
made headlines for the dailies, Page A1.

I begin to think she was mine. Leaflets
aging on store fronts show date missed,
her eyes and hair, REWARD FOR SAFE RETURN.
Police with dogs search the Raritan

for the published coat *last seen*
for the form *female, matching description*

5.

Speak of the peace, its strangeness, a country
seen first at dusk. Of the plane tree
not taking its shape back from the dark yet.
Speak of the wet pad spots tracked to the bed
and the wrung towels thrown and the two soup bowls.
And of the chests and hips, slightly apart, to cool.
And of the great, great quiet, the wordless lips
shaping only the many shapes of kisses.
And the slackened legs and back stroked for their work.
And the near-sleep shiftings, and lone work
steps of the first on the sidewalk. Then daylight came
the way a dancer will begin lifting her arms
and lift them without any music. I kept
one hand on your chest, whether I woke or slept.

6.

I squat beside a crate that stays buried
in what won't go elsewhere: notebook
I bought in '88 to hold my worries,
slides of the Rhineland (borrowed). Near work

I took this pamphlet: *The First Nine Months*
with photos. Barricaded, rubbing prayer beads
one shrieked *she rips babies from their mothers*
To the near-girl, going in, *miss, please miss, please*

At school, one child less: Miss Charlene sent
the oldest (reads the note) to foster care.
She's taken three in from her children,
writes here *too much with this one more*

I study the paddle hands, mud bit of eye,
gauze sac across the face. And want that child.

7.

The title's Brooklyn's, of thin floor and wall,
of Sunday's *hate-you-fuck-you-listening?-I'll
leave!* They didn't. Not the new ones down the hall,

the landlord and wife who'd kept it up for years.
Mid-block, ROMEO COLLISION could repair
what broke an auto body. The title's yours:

Quick step across the stoop, quick look up
to see if I looked. Fear or love?
Which is it moving us who move

the way the tamer steps in the cage, alone—
(In the air above your coat you drew cartoon
hearts, great bursting ones. Then came in.)

who say *Beloved.* Lay out the wrapped
pears, two colors of flowers. Who accept.

IV

# THE CICADAS

Of constant things, they are most constant,
inciting memory, never the thing remembered
but the attendant, bordering the way into memory,
girls strewing petals the day of the wedding

within veils of wings. Hear the pattern to the confusion:
something fumbled for, and dropped, and fumbled for,
the right bead slipped on a string. A thread apparent,
a limb. The summer night is always dimmed

by the woman in her slip at the window,
car headlights on the dark stain of the river
that extinguish, and other light scattered on the river
the way memory obstructs a certain dark—

The ring of children has scattered. They hide
and glitter, small lungs spreading, folding.
Already the first call back *safe! home!*
Now you can bear to remember what you

could bear to do once, carried by breathing
so like this music, in which what you lose, recurs.
The scale of the night slowly fills with petals,
leaves edged in weak light, the laboring wings.

# THE GRAVEYARD

1.

North of here the mountains start—
each one bigger than the one before:
bigger than all the heavings to drums,
than the noises of deep drum throats
                 to the stories of giants.

A giant passed through a town.
Of the townspeople fated
(let us say *fated*)
to be on the streets that day,
thirty were taken, slain,
and robbed to meet a bet.
Thirty lay naked
through that town, in various attitudes,
some open-mouthed, as though speech would return to them.

2.

There is nobody in the graveyard, nobody at all,
though it rises like a white city one approaches,
towers with no watchmen, but the stillness of watching.

The graveyard suggests many things:
that a wind might rise
that a wind is rising
that there are doings on the sea floor
same as here, shift and scuttle
that leaves wear fast, stone rounds slowly

and the Nesbits and Mills are neighbors
and the Mussers and names not used anymore.

The ground with its shiftings disturbs some
makes their attitudes more like falling or climbing.
The cold wind is early this year, an assassin.

There is nobody. Not blessed, not cursed,
neither sleeping nor speaking
nor minding the patterns of any stars,
neither greater than one, nor less:
not one in the manner of a person
but one in the manner of a city.

3.

Who will mourn her, that met her father with timbrels and dancing?
The young virgins mourned:
they went each year into the mountain
at the time of the year she was slaughtered
for the good name of her father's house.
She accepted. Who will mourn her?

4.

Now a boy with a football stretching his T-shirt neck
rides his bicycle with its slamming noise between grave markers,
some rough-cut, some spotted as with precious blood,
carved haunch, lamb, carved fruit and rose.

Not undone. We are gathered
in the manner of a city.

My violent and amending hands.
Different people saying truthfully
*That dog is dangerous. No, that dog is a good one.*
Before that, in the morning, my kind self
gets and lifts up my hurting self.
White block trucks unload in the market
below the crone, perpetually half behind a curtain;
the wrong side of town leans further toward undoing.
Young men, balanced between howl and purpose,
emerge from businesses into the noon.
The young wife hangs her cage of birds.
The mother, exclaiming, tears bread for the ducks
and the hands of the child reach for the ducks
uncertainly, as if releasing a wobbly bright ball.

# DOG DAYS

*for Ann and Jean, finishing dissertations*

I mind I've been an hour beside shut books,
or more. The wind moves almost nothing
in trees that move like a heavy woman
I once saw blowing kisses. All work
suspends: tomatoes shine on the wiped table
from noon gardens. Grain stands in the fields.

Summer was a dream that broke. Memory's fields
mark this a time of loss. I've lived off books
while locusts husk a last call and the table
piles with clothes to store. Nothing
ends easily as this season, work
of the round year. When I was not a woman,

quite, my sixteenth year, like a woman,
I swam alone once in a river. The fields
touched into August evening in its work
toward September. The moon came out. In books
a moon required lovers. I wanted nothing
but to give a woman's love, sturdy, like a table,

weight-bearing. We sat across a table,
drank and forgot the hour, spoke woman-
to-woman about an anger. She said, "nothing
tires me like the old boys: men teaching men fields
of knowledge. Xanthippe sent off crying." Books
to come, we toasted those, an audience, our work.

Drink deceives, but so does work:
at best it passes time. Idling at the table
I've known what the Preacher set in books
as a truth: for child of woman
(I paraphrase), what labor, in actual fields,
or of the mind, satisfies? We come to nothing.

I stare at trees in wind and finish nothing
but hours. I think of two who work,
dear to me, shut in, as sick for fields,
perhaps, as I for work. Along a table
sun whitens a lax arm. The woman
admires the tiny hairs, forgets books.

She forgets the fields and laden table
that soon hold nothing, while birds work
south across a woman and shut books.

# THE SIMPLE DAY

I rise up with my breasts, bubble and seed,
smaller than nationally advertised breasts.
I rise up with my ribs spreading
like the tusks of clouds at evening,
I rise up with my fists, which came before the hand.
Then fists and mouth open. I don't remember
getting down the stairs.
This is the hour some light their first smoke
off the stove eye,
pajamas drooping below the butt.
We're like actors offstage
before the performance, the disastrous one.
But we're calm. I step onto the porch.
Back mountain's gone. Rain.

The clock hangs crooked. But time comes on
the same. Strike. No reason to wake.
One wants to make a tunnel
shaped like the reclining body, one likes
to lie under something and hear rain.
She comes to the door in a yellow robe,
her eyes with their milky newborn-color cataracts
not focused. I woke you, I say, shake
out my umbrella, go.

Rain makes a home, it rounds
the light above our heads. The child drinks
so greedily he forgets to breathe,
gasps as he sucks.
There will be soup for dinner,
and the kitten is healing.
I make a tunnel, says the child.
I don't understand. Tun! tun! tunna!
he grows distressed: it had been my word.

The day stays dark as evening
in a town street before lamps are lit
and all who walk there think, *home*.
The blond leaves grow dark, take on
the suggestion of rotting. Some
fell twice: to roofs, then blew
off roofs into the chattering air.
Sleep is near. The eyelids swell
like acorn caps, want to drop.

Where are the warriors, table thumpers,
voices of the masses? The presses clicking,
cap guns clicking? Where is the Carnival parade,
the sequined and the striped leg,
wink of the stripper and pantomime of stripper?
Not in the simple day. I sigh,
step back out of my pajamas.
Skin slouches, like pajamas.

# LEAVING NEW YORK CITY

Two hours in a dented van to Trenton,
Calhoun Street Bridge. The Delaware's down,
sunk to the last of itself,
snaky with grasses underneath,
little gold dome of the capitol like a filled tooth.
Let not what I have be taken from me,
but let me step new from *was* into *is*.

My arms hurt with the long hurt of lifting,
all things on me that lift, all blades
and notched belts ticking upwards, they hurt,
and the ass which spreads and clamps to climb,
and my legs hurt with the chipped hurts of stairs.
"Your problem, not mine," the landlord sat
down to his dinner, the new tenant smirked.
I boxed everything, also hopes that went wrong,
sewing patterns, the lover's clothes.
I'm pulling out. I was never in.
New York, you'd stop my heart
each time on top of the subway stairs.

If I admire my knees, the knobs on the inner side,
the fact that they bend, the act of their bending,
if I admire the toes that grip
the floor in argument against the falling body,
or I admire the turning head and fixed spine,
energy flashlighting forever out the top,
I will have enough.

I haven't learned maintenance, the sitting still and breathing.
My modes are forwards, backwards (which is fixing)
and debauchery, the long fall.
One of my ancestors fell. I dream the *thump:*
I gather in my bones,
my breath goes *ha,* and then I hit.

# ABOUT THE PELVIS

Pelvis, that furnace, is a self-fueler:
shoveler of energy into the body.

It is the chair that walks. Swing
that can fire off like a rocket.

It carries the torso, it sets the torso down.
It connects the brother legs, and lets them speak.

Trust the pelvis—it will get everything else there:
pull you onto a ledge, push you into a run.

It is the other spine, prone, like the fallow field.
Here are the constellations of the pelvis:

Drawn Bow, Flame-of-One-Branch,
Round Star, and Down-Hanging-Mountains.

Here is the dress of the pelvis: crescent belly,
and buttocks shaken like a dance of masks.

Forget the pelvis, and you're a stove good for parts:
motion gone, heat gone, and the soup pots empty.

## FOR NAJEEMA, 6, WHO ADMITTED TO HITTING RENEE

Trenton told you before the teacher did,
*people do bad things*
*if they start touching people*

But girl, our hands have more touches
than shapes waiting to get out of wood:
a bucked dancer or a floating bird

Your hands have more ways
than kinds of animals came
out of Noah's ark: you have

touches for the faces of the blind
touches especially for the heads of children
touches so new they're hiding in
your hands, Najeema. Go lay them on.

# BROTHER ASS

### 1.

Socrates, unfettered for a few, last, hours,
rubbed his legs and spoke of the body's ills
which his kind must ignore:
he meant the five senses. Do you know

how the soul's fetters are said to look?
Two eyes, two thumbs, shocks of hair
below and above, and it walks
with the gait your mama gave you.

### 2.

Its crimes as follows: wasting,
dying. Rotting. Stinking also in life,
possessing pits, possessing mucus. Lusting.
Rooting in stinks: lumbering after
the reeking ovens of other bodies
dragging the undefended spirit
to all manner of high school parties and back rooms
where squint-eyed women line up pool shots
and call each other *bitch*. And there teeters the body,
grinning, beer foam on its teeth:
it will not be the one sent to hell fire to burn.

But how will we tame it? Shall we make it kneel?
Make it celibate, starve it, as the dancer wastes and hardens hers?
Whip it through long marches like the flagellants
who thought to stop the plague?

### 3.

Or is it the body that is first of all wise? My arthritic aunt
is visited all afternoon in her fan-stirred living room
by neighbors wanting advice
for she took over what her failing body knew.

The body does not fear: that is the chattering soul's.
The body knows hurt: it pulls its hand from the flame.
It covers its backside with a blanket in the cold wind.
It would not charge the bayoneted enemy line.
It neither rules nor follows, nor cares to teach:
it is merely the bear and the paw at the crack of honey.

# COURAGE, OR ONE OF GENE HORNER'S FIDDLES

After I write *My face burned and I wanted to cry*
I watch Catherine Osborn, who was on oxygen all winter,
walk slowly by the canal, with the jerking motions of a small boat
when the people in it move or change places on their knees.
*You don't know nothing. Do you?* Gene had said.
I had come to see about buying a fiddle.
Rainy day, the Cumberlands blunting any notion of future.
*Well,* I said. My face burned and I wanted to cry.
Then he played for me, he would have played for anyone,
a dark maple fiddle he'd made, such a pure sound
it could have belonged to either of us,
it seemed to rise from the frets of my wrists, my curled hands.
We are wrong about courage. It is closer to music.
It rises from us simply as we move in this life, or submit.

# IN TROUT SEASON

So I take my breath and clay self
down to the canal path that wears through
its tracks of who used to go there:
gone mule and the boy who drove her,
and the scuff-heeled loiterer turning
full in the noon sun who felt, oh,
the dark shape of his heart like a treasure.

Some of us fear beauty:
the double pride curl of the duck's tail
or the first buds spread in a sheerness
like the veil the new bride lies in,
the one thing she wears.

Now the trout fishers are in season
and have crowded the bank
with their mild, identical hopes
to squat in makeshift shade:
some inked by the tattoo needle
more colors than pattern trout,
some with a child alongside, tensed
to begin pointing or fetch,
some with the fisherman's stare
of beginning to go over
what had nearly no longer mattered.
And the line completing their waiting
barely there—
as prayers might look in ascension
on a wire for carrying prayers
or as the spirit shines when it extends
in ecstasy past the body
but walks on with the body. Or sits, fishing.

# FOR SHEILA'S JULIA

You riding in circles a made-up horse
or chalking animals beside your house
*while briar unchecked ravels over briar*
a heaped-on dark, hiding snakes or worse—

you look, if you look, on hills that will move
with your life to ring it, the way those you love
*while briar unchecked ravels over briar*
will stay to love you. Or so you believe.

I watch you slide on gravel with your bike
and frown through hair whitish like milk
*while briar unchecked ravels over briar*
your chest with but a fiddle case's bulk

then, Julia, it seems all that I've learned
would fit into the song born-broken-born
*while briar unchecked ravels over briar.*
For your sake I love this: born-broken-born.

# NOTES

"Pulled Down" is taken from interviews with Mae Storey and Maggie Barger about Glenmary, Tennessee—where my mother was born—in its boom time. "Glenmary, 1990" is based on remembrances about the family homeplace by my mother's eldest sister, Lois Wright Hixon. I first visited Glenmary in 1990, the last year the family house was standing.

"The Road to Canso" and "In Fraser's Mills" are set in Nova Scotia. Fraser's Mills is an area settled by Scots immigrants.

"Products of Hogs" uses information from the book *Sketches and Statistics of Cincinnati* (1851).

"Brother Ass" is the fairly affectionate name Saint Francis of Assisi is said to have used for the body.